Thank you for choosing
this book,
Mihaela Dodan

With love, to Lyra Arabella and all
the children of this world.

ISBN: 978-0-578-18113-4
Library of Congress Control Number: 2016909962

www.mihaeladodan.com
www.magicmindcollection.com

Magic Choices

Where your mind is, your reality is.

Lyra! Mommy called, smiling warmly.
Yes, Mommy? Lyra asked.

It is time for you to know something important about your life.
What is it? Lyra asked curiously, running to her mother.

As you grow, Lyra, a magic garden also grows in your mind. It will provide everything you choose to experience.

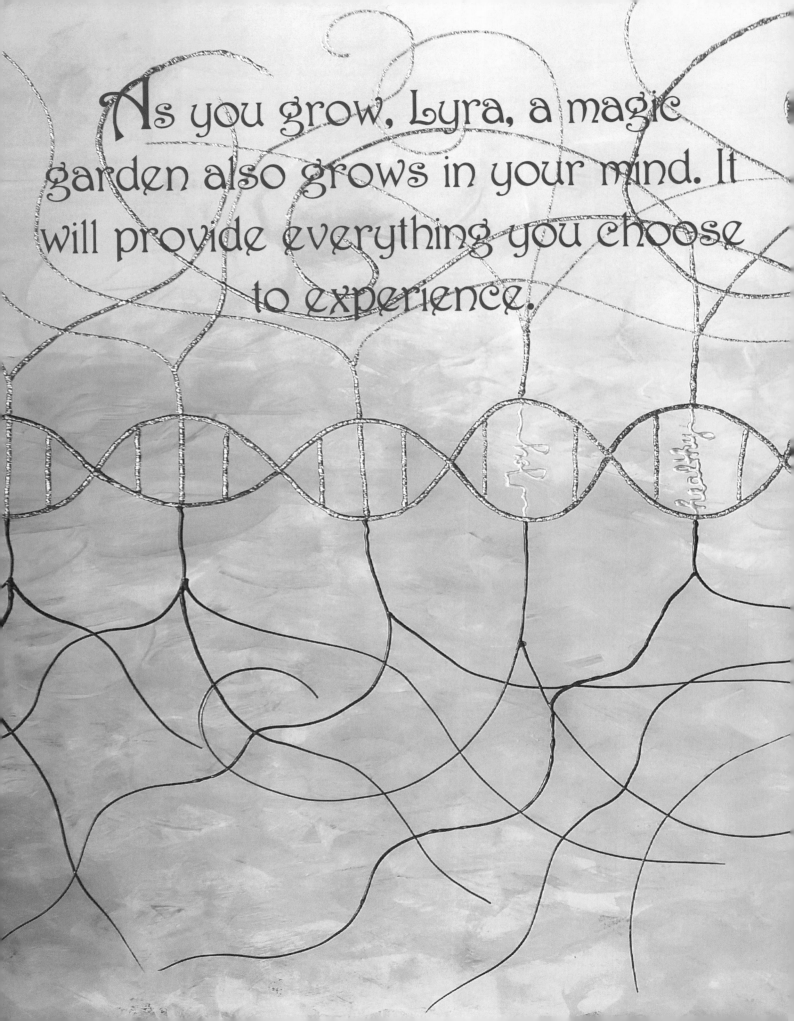

Being a mind garden, the plants will start from magic, sparkly seeds that only you can choose.

Where can we buy some sparkly seeds?
I love sparkles! Lyra exclaimed.

These seeds are
invisible, but they will
sparkle in your mind.
They are available to
all people, for free.
We only need to
choose them in our
minds. We bathe in an
infinite ocean of
sparkly seeds, all the
time.

What do you mean? What are they?

I am the seed of joy!
Pick me, pick me!

I am the seed of love!
Pick me too!

I am the seed of creativity.
I want to grow and make beautiful things.

...Harmony, Kindness, Honesty, Wisdom,
Energy,

I am the seed of genius! Pick me!

I am the seed of
wealth. Pick me!

I am the seed of health. Pick me,
I will help you grow into all of
your dreams!

Clarity, Generosity, Compassion, Strength,
Persistence...

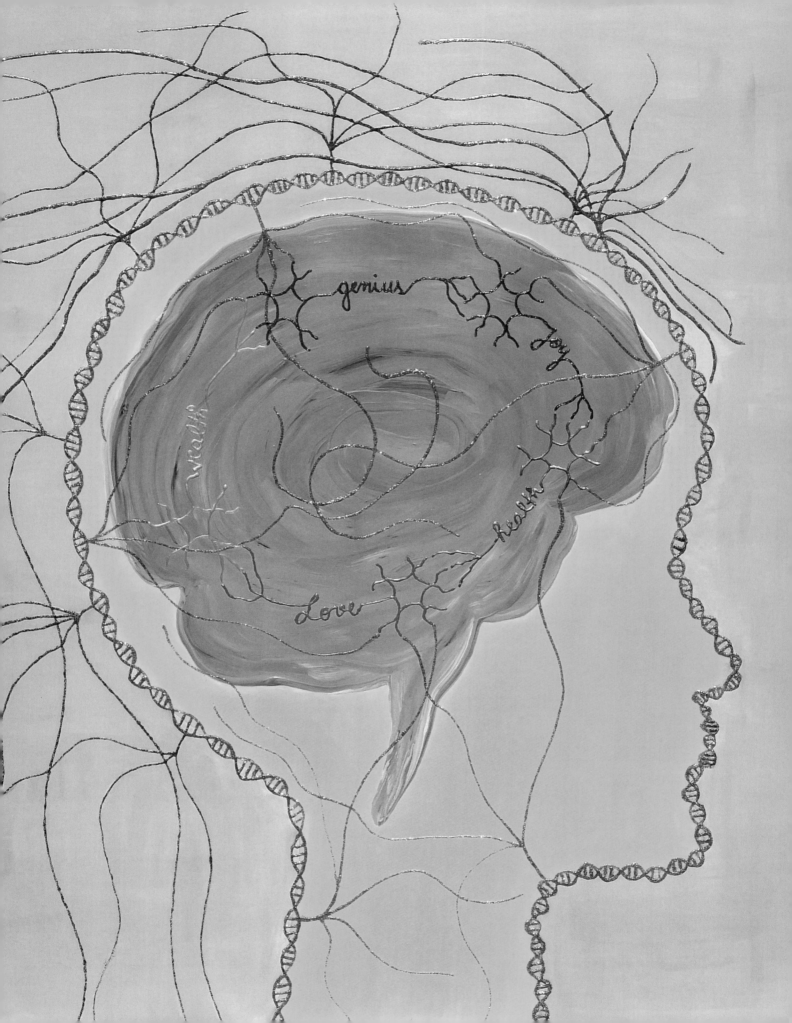

wealth

health

love

It is fun and magic and wondrous and sparkly to care for your mind and everything that grows inside of it.
You can explore and make new choices at any moment. That is a freedom we all have. If a seed got inside and you do not like it, you can choose to give it up! Gently move your mind to other choices, other seeds you want to grow.

genius

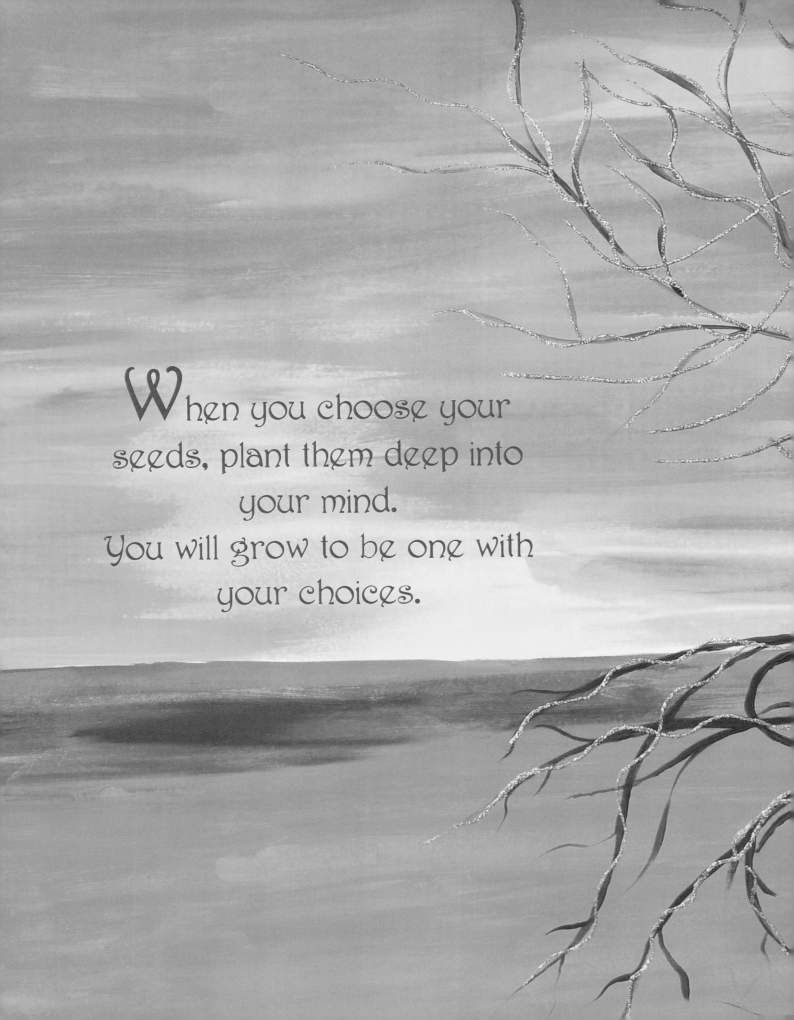

When you choose your seeds, plant them deep into your mind.
You will grow to be one with your choices.

Mommy, how do these seeds grow
in my mind? What do I do?
What do you mean?
I am glad you asked, said Mommy.
One of the most important keys to
learning what you can be, do, and have
is to ask questions. That is the
beginning of every adventure.

Let's play with seeds of love, said Mommy.
When you think
about love, it
already starts
to grow with you.
You start to feel it
in your body. It is
sweet and soft and
warm and fuzzy.
Do you feel it?

Yes, it's ticklish inside my belly! Lyra giggled.
As you wonder about love, your mind will come up with many ideas about how to love. You will start to see love everywhere.

Remember how we write in the morning what we want the day to be like?
Yes, said Lyra, thinking of Mommy writing and drawing in her notebook.
That's part of taking care of your mind garden.

Another way to care for your mind
is to create a vision board
where you can draw your sparkly
choices. That way, your seeds
are always in your attention and they
grow with you.

If you ever find that you are not enjoying yourself, stop and check what is happening in your magic garden. Choose again how you want to feel, what you want to be, or what you want to explore.

YOU GET TO CHOOSE!

Always explore. Always be open to new seeds, new possibilities.

There are many other keys for a magic mind and I will share them with you, step by step.

For now, use these first ones:

Ask questions.

Draw and write what you want to be, to do, and to have.

Make a vision board picturing your choices.

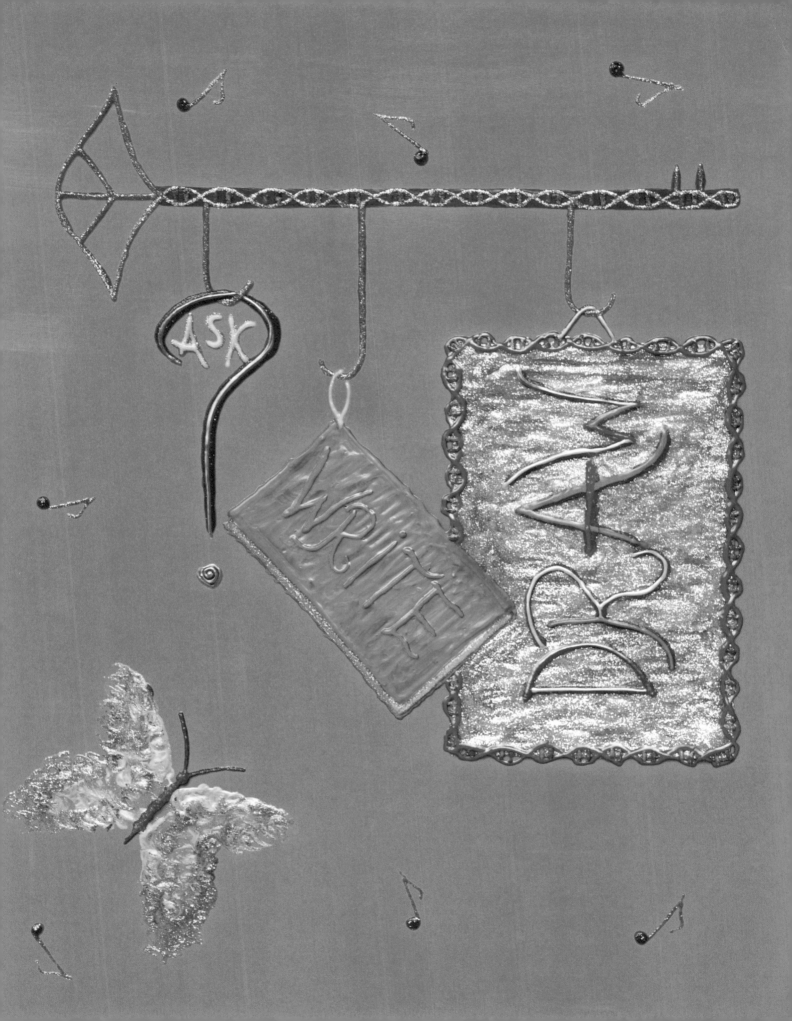

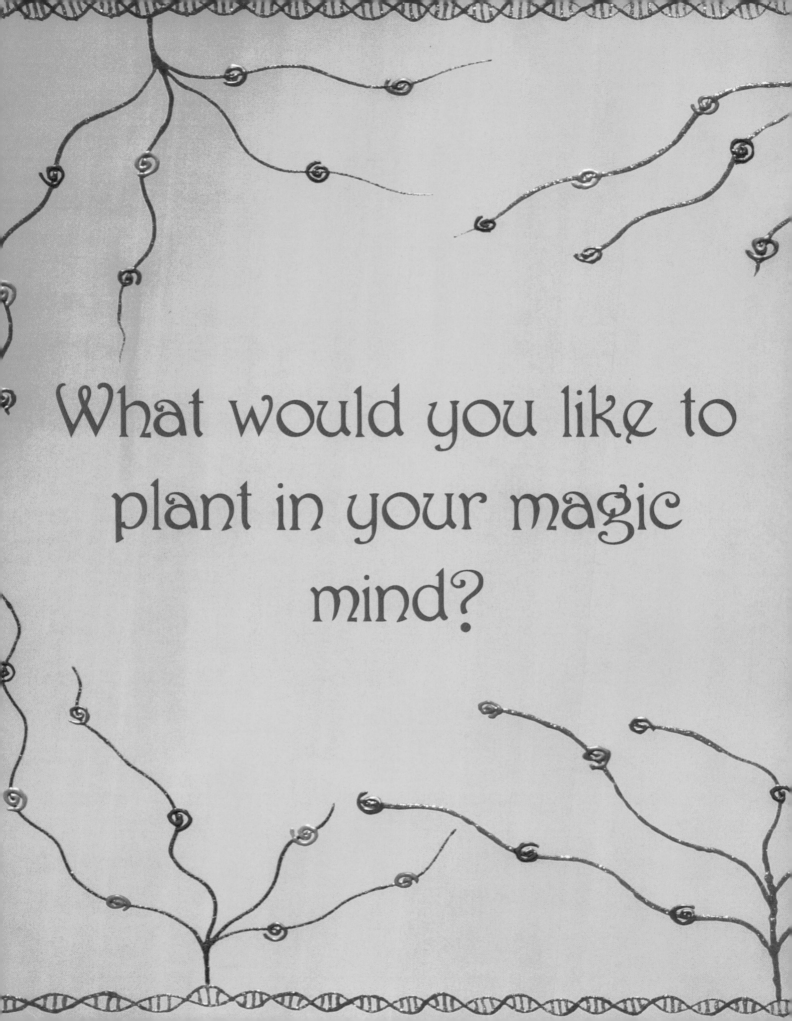

What would you like to plant in your magic mind?

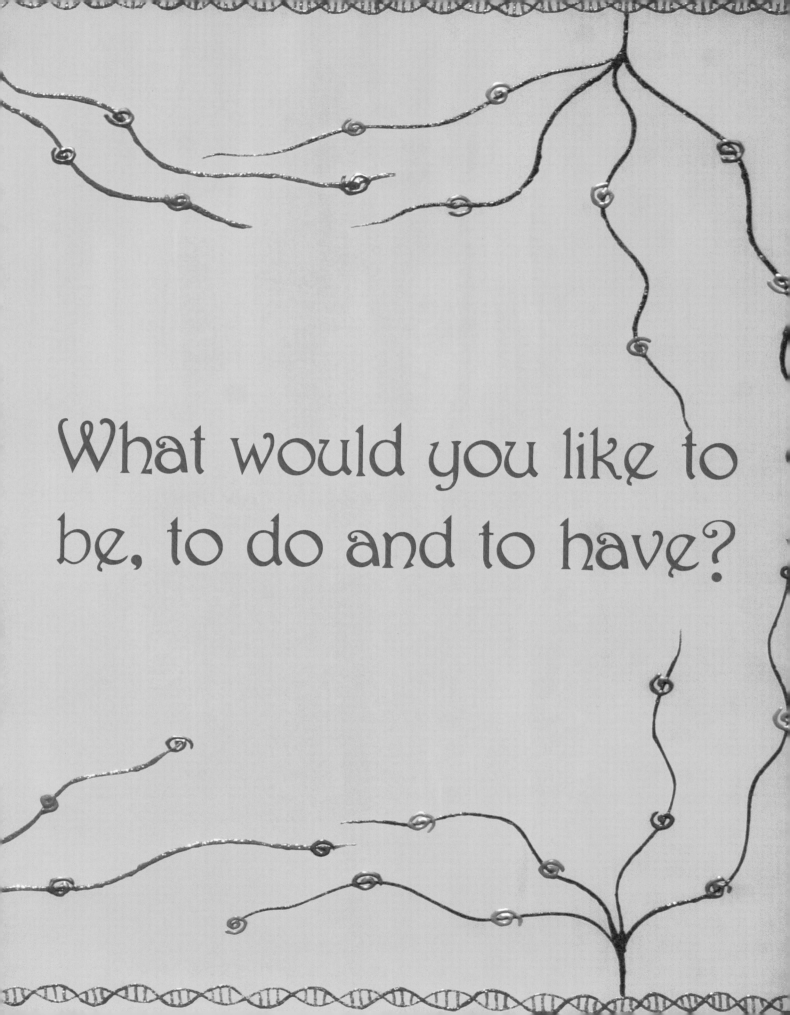

What would you like to be, to do and to have?

About Mihaela

I was born and raised in Romania with my four brothers during a very dark Communist era. I learned (often by the light of a candle) from cooking, cleaning, knitting, babysitting, how to open a can with a knife before I was seven to all the disciplines children learn in school.

At 22, after graduating college, I left Romania to work on cruise ships. That was an intense training on how to communicate with passengers; take care of their luggage and quarters; deal with paperwork and safety in a floating city; and manage countless other duties.

After five years of work aboard ships, I built a farm in Romania, I participated in building a meat-processing factory, and I started a publishing company.

Despite all this experience, I found myself not understanding the purpose of life. Wondering about it all, I set myself on a whole new course of learning, unlearning, and self-revealing.

In 2006, while still in Europe, I began to learn and practice energy healing techniques, Hypnosis, Neuro-Linguistic Programming (NLP), Mind Control, Life and Business Coaching, Health Coaching, and more.

In 2010 I moved to the United States to study at RSE, in Yelm, WA. I have become even more passionate to know about the power of mind over matter.

In 2014 I graduated from the Institute of Integrative Nutrition, NY, as a Health Coach.

Somewhere in between I discovered my passion for writing and painting.

Lyra Arabella is a fairly new citizen of Planet Earth. Like all citizens on this planet, she will be taught how to navigate and live her life.

I, her mommy, decided to create a series of short and simple books to pass on to Lyra, and those who find it useful, what I have learned so far.

Acknowledgments

I'm deeply grateful to my parents. I
continuously open my eyes to the
immeasurable efforts they made for me and
my brothers to have more
possibilities in life.
I'm grateful to my daughter for her
presence and all the gifts she brings into
my life.
I'm grateful to JZ Knight and Ramtha for
giving me a whole new set of magic, sparkly
seeds to plant in my mind, and for helping
me grow with them into
possibilities I couldn't even think of, before
meeting them.
I am grateful to myself, for taking
on this journey!

Other Magic Books to come:

Magic Luggage

Magic Thoughts

Magic Words

Magic Chocolate

Magic Nutrients

Magic Questions

Magic Invisibility

And more

Lightning Source UK Ltd.
Milton Keynes UK
UKRC010427071118
331894UK00005B/121